In Her Stride

Written by Peter Rees
Illustrated by Margaret Power

U.S.A.

Contents

Who Is Loretta Claiborne?

Loretta Claiborne is an athlete and a spokesperson for the global Special Olympics movement. She has overcome physical and intellectual challenges to become a popular public speaker and role model for others with disabilities. Loretta has often been featured in books, on TV, and on radio. Her life story carries an inspiring message of hope and tolerance for people around the world.

In this interview, Loretta describes with honesty and humor her early struggles and her successes.

August 14, 1953
Loretta Claiborne is born in York, Pennsylvania.

1966
Loretta begins running with her brother Hank.

1970
Loretta attends her first Special Olympics track meet.

1982
Loretta joins the board of Special Olympics Pennsylvania. She places among the top 100 women in the Boston Marathon for the second time.

Setting the Scene

York, Pennsylvania

Loretta comes from the city of York, Pennsylvania. York is a historic city that was the first capital of the United States. For a child growing up there in the 1950s and 1960s, York was not always a safe place to be. Tensions between people of different races sometimes led to violence and rioting.

Chicago, IL

York, PA

U.S.A.

Washington, D.C.

Baton Rouge, LA

1983	1990	1996	2000
Loretta wins her first gold medal at the Special Olympics International Games in Baton Rouge, Louisiana.	Loretta becomes a member of the board of Special Olympics International.	Loretta is awarded the Arthur Ashe Courage Award.	A film, *The Loretta Claiborne Story*, is made about Loretta's life.

Growing Up Different

Q: Loretta, you grew up with an intellectual disability. When did you first realize you were different from most other children?

A: *I was nine years old. At my school, young people were able to go and sign up to be on the safety patrol. I wanted to sign up, too, but my class was a special-education class, and we weren't allowed to do those kinds of things. So my hopes of being on the safety patrol were dashed. Even though I had dreams of being an athlete and dreams of being a nurse, I knew my dreams wouldn't come true.*

intellectual disability learning difficulties

> *"I just wanted to do what everybody else did, and I was always pushed aside."*
> **—Loretta Claiborne**

Loretta Claiborne was born on August 14, 1953, the middle child of seven. She lived with her mother and her brothers and sisters in a housing project in York, Pennsylvania. Loretta was born with impaired sight and a mild intellectual disability, which meant she wasn't able to walk or talk until she was four. Because of her disability, she was often teased and bullied at school.

Loretta at age 6

housing project an area of housing for low-income families

Fighting Back

Q: How did it make you feel when some of the other children teased you?

A: *I felt bad. I felt angry, and I fought back with my fists. Fighting was my only tool, because there was no point in talking. I would always be told, "We don't want to hear what you have to say—you don't know anything!"*

We lived in a big housing project. It was like being in a jungle; you had to fight to survive. I would come home crying, and my mom would say, "Go back out there and deal with it the best way you can."

"Two things I could do well were fight and run."
—Loretta Claiborne

Loretta's quick temper sometimes got her into trouble with school authorities. Many of her problems were caused by her feelings of low self-esteem. To help Loretta feel better about herself, doctors operated to straighten her eyes, which had been crossed since she was born. They also fixed bones in her right foot, enabling her to walk more easily.

Loretta (far left) with her sisters, Debbie, Van, and Stella

self-esteem feeling confident about yourself

9

On the Run

Q: When did you discover you had athletic ability?

A: *I started running with my brother Hank when I was twelve years old. As time went by, I just kept running and running. I would run around the housing projects. It was something I could do by myself, and kids didn't tease me.*

Once, some girls at school got together and decided to have a track team. I wanted to be a part of it. I even collected money for it. Some of the other girls didn't want a person with an intellectual disability on the team, but the coach said, "Loretta has just as much right to be on this team as any of you."

At the time Loretta attended school, girls often did not have the same opportunities to play sports as boys. Loretta's all-girl track team was not even allowed to practice on the school running track, which was reserved for boys. It wasn't until 1972 that a law was passed in the United States giving all children the same right to play sports.

Loretta (left) with her school track team

Special Olympics

Q: How did you become involved with Special Olympics?

A: *By the time I was in high school, anger had become my way of getting through life. I didn't want anyone to bother me. I just wanted to come home from school every day and be my angry self.*

In those days, I was working part time at a sheltered workshop. I used to run from home to the workshop, even though there was a free bus. A counselor at the workshop saw me running and suggested I go to a Special Olympics track meet. At first, I didn't want to go! I didn't think they'd want a "retard" from the projects—that's how I saw myself.

sheltered workshop a place where people with disabilities make products and crafts for sale

Special Olympics was created to give people with intellectual disabilities the opportunity to compete against each other in sports. All year long, Special Olympics helps organize games and sporting events for intellectually challenged athletes in more than 150 countries.

Winners of national events go to the Special Olympics World Summer and Winter Games, now held every four years. The First International Special Olympics Games were held in July 1968 in Chicago, Illinois.

The opening of the First Special Olympics Games in 1968

"Blooming and Growing"

Q: How did becoming a part of Special Olympics change your life?

A: *It made me put down my fists and start to use my head and my feet. I began making my own decisions. One decision I made was to learn sign language so I could communicate with deaf people at the workshop. Another was to take a self-defense class and learn karate. It took me a long time to learn something, but once I did, I never forgot it. Eventually I became a fourth-degree black belt in karate. Now I teach karate—not only to people with intellectual disabilities, but to all kinds of people.*

Loretta graduated from high school in 1972. Since then, she has continued to seek out new learning opportunities. In addition to earning a black belt in karate, Loretta has learned four languages, including sign language. She is the only person with an intellectual disability to receive honorary doctorates from two universities.

Loretta received an honorary Doctor of Humane Letters degree from Villanova University in 2003.

honorary given as an honor

Winning

Q: Tell us about the time you won your first big race.

A: *In 1983, the International Special Olympics Games were held in Baton Rouge, Louisiana. I trained a lot before the Games. Every day I went to the gym, and then I ran on the road for five or six miles. It didn't matter what the weather was like; rain, snow, sleet, and hail—I ran through it all.*

My race was the mile. The race started, but before long a girl next to me almost tripped me up. I was so mad, I took off like a jack rabbit. That was how I won my first gold medal! There are no words for how it felt.

"I guess if there's a word better than 'fantastic,' it felt better than fantastic!"
—Loretta on winning her first gold medal

The Sixth International Special Olympics Summer Games at Baton Rouge, Louisiana, were the largest that had been held. More than 4,000 athletes competed at the Games, and at least 60,000 spectators watched the opening ceremony.

Each year, the number of Special Olympics athletes and spectators continues to grow. In 2003, 7,000 athletes from more than 150 countries participated at the World Summer Games in Dublin, Ireland.

Runners compete in a relay race at the 2003 World Summer Games in Dublin.

The Marathon Bug

Q: You also had another interest—running in marathons. How did that begin?

A: *I started running in marathons in 1978 with my friend Bob. The best experience was the first, because we didn't know what we were getting into. I said to Bob, "This book says that a marathon is 26.2 miles—that sounds like a long way!" Bob said, "That's OK. We'll train for it."*

The day of the race came. About halfway, I got a huge blister. I was half running and half hobbling. Even so, I ran a good time for a first marathon. After that, I got the marathon bug, although Bob didn't—it was his first and last marathon!

marathon   a race run on roads
that is 26.2 miles long

Since her first marathon in Harrisburg, Pennsylvania, Loretta has run 26 marathons, one for every mile of the marathon distance! In 1981 and 1982, Loretta placed among the top 100 women in the world-famous Boston Marathon in the United States.

Loretta was the first woman to cross the finish line in the 1985 Red Rose Run in Lancaster, Pennsylvania.

Global Messenger

Q: Tell us about your latest role with Special Olympics.

A: *For a long time, I served on the boards of directors of Special Olympics in Washington, D.C., and Pennsylvania. I was asked to join the boards to speak on behalf of the athletes. Now I'm a Global Messenger for Special Olympics. My job is to go out and help build support for Special Olympics. I travel to different countries and speak to all kinds of groups.*

We have many Global Messengers all around the world. I'm just one of them. Special Olympics is a global movement. We're changing negative attitudes about people with intellectual disabilities.

board   a group of people who make decisions about an organization

"We can start changing the world by changing one attitude at a time."
—Loretta Claiborne

In 1982, Loretta became the first athlete to serve on the board of Special Olympics Pennsylvania. She joined the Special Olympics International Board in 1990 and served on it for 11 years. In her time as a Global Messenger for Special Olympics, Loretta has addressed numerous gatherings and met many leaders and sports figures around the world.

Loretta is shown here with friends, including former South African president Nelson Mandela (second from left) and Special Olympics Global Ambassador Arnold Schwarzenegger (second from right), while on a visit to South Africa in 2001.

A Good Run

Like many people with an intellectual disability, Loretta grew up being told what she couldn't do. She proved all her doubters wrong. Now in her 50s, she still trains every day and plans to keep running for as long as she can. She travels widely, giving interviews and speaking at functions in support of Special Olympics. In 2000, there was even a movie made about her life.

Loretta's proudest moment was receiving the Arthur Ashe Courage Award in 1996. She joined a small group of outstanding figures from the world of sports who have been honored in this way.

Sporting Heroes

The Arthur Ashe Courage Award is a yearly award given to a sports figure who has made an important contribution to the world. It is named after Arthur Ashe (1943–1993), an African American who overcame racial prejudice to become one of the world's best tennis players. Others who have received the award include:

- Muhammad Ali (U.S. boxer, 1997)

- Billie Jean King (U.S. tennis player, 1999)

- Cathy Freeman (Australian runner, 2001)

- Pat Tillman (U.S. football player, 2003) and Kevin Tillman (U.S. baseball player, 2003)

- George Weah (Liberian soccer player, 2004)

What If?

Loretta was fortunate that her natural abilities were recognized and encouraged by those around her. Thanks to her involvement in Special Olympics, she was able to take responsibility for her own actions and achieve her full potential. What if Loretta had continued on the path of anger and violence? How might her life be different today?

Loretta showed her determination to compete by putting in long hours of training. How do you show determination in your life?

Index

determination a drive to succeed